THE
SAILOR
THROUGH HISTORY

Roger Coote

with illustrations by Tony Smith

Thomson Learning
New York

JOURNEY THROUGH HISTORY
The Builder Through History
The Explorer Through History
The Farmer Through History
The Inventor Through History
The Sailor Through History
The Soldier Through History

First published in the
United States in 1993 by
Thomson Learning
115 Fifth Avenue
New York, NY 10003

First published in 1993 by
Wayland (Publishers) Ltd
61 Western Road, Hove
East Sussex, BN3 1JD, England

**Cataloging-in-Publication Data
Applied For.**

ISBN 1-56847-012-6

Printed in Italy.

Picture acknowledgments
The publishers would like to thank
the following for permission to
reproduce their pictures: Ancient Art
and Architecture Collection 12, 14;
British Museum 15 bottom; ET
Archive 10, 22, 28 bottom; Mary
Evans 18; Michael Holford 8;
Mansell Collection 4 top, 13, 25 26,
36 top, 37 bottom; Peter Newark's
Pictures 16, 28 top, 32, 33, 37 top,
40; Photri 20, 38; The Research
House 4 bottom; Science Museum
30, 34, 36, bottom; Shell UK 42;
Topham Picture Source 15 top, 41,
44 bottom; ZEFA 5, 9, 44 top, 45.

The illustration on page 40 is by
Peter Bull; all other illustrations are
by Tony Smith.

Contents

Ships and the sea

Ships and sailors have played an important part in the history of civilization. They made possible the exploration of vast areas of our world. In some cases, they enabled people to settle in regions that were previously uninhabited and could only be reached by boat. This is how the Polynesians came to settle on remote islands of the Pacific Ocean. The colonies founded several centuries ago by Spain, Portugal, Britain, and other countries owed their existence to the sailors who traveled there and took supplies to the colonists. Throughout history, ships have been used for military purposes — for attacking other ships and carrying invasion forces. The technically advanced ships and highly trained sailors of modern navies show that this role is still important.

Exploration, conquest, and colonization almost always brought something else in their wake — trade.

Above The Portuguese sailor Bartholomew Diaz sailed to the southern tip of Africa in 1487.

Below A U.S. Navy aircraft carrier. Ships have been used for warfare for many centuries.

Coffee is loaded on to a merchant ship in Brazil.

Until quite recently, ships were the only means of transporting large quantities of goods over long distances. Railways, trucks, and aircraft have reduced the importance of ships as cargo-carriers but, even today, many large, heavy cargoes are sent by sea because it is the cheapest method. Crude oil is one example. Huge supertankers only need the same number of crew as smaller ships, yet can carry much more oil. They have reduced the cost of transporting oil around the world.

The earliest ships were powered by oars, paddles, and sails. Within the last 150 years, other forms of power have become widely available. The first innovation was the steam engine. It brought to an end the days of large ships driven by the wind in their sails. Improvements in the design of steam engines and steam ships provided more power and greater speed, and brought in the age of the great ocean-going liners. They in turn were superseded by jet aircraft, which can travel many times faster than even the fastest ship.

Perhaps the most important part of any ship is the crew who sail it. Throughout history, almost all crews were made up of men. That is not to say that women did not take sea voyages. Women and children traveled as colonists — Polynesian women crossed vast oceans in canoes, European women sailed across the Atlantic to America, and there were even some women pirates. Today, there are thousands of women sailors — on warships, merchant ships, and yachts.

Until recently, life at sea was often uncomfortable and dangerous. Sailors had to deal with poor food, little warmth or shelter, risks of shipwreck or battle, and, on long journeys, the risk of catching a fatal disease. In many cases they were also very fearful of the unknown waters onto which they sailed. Today, many of these problems have been overcome, now that ships are stronger and better equipped and the seas are well charted. Even so, they are still at the mercy of the sea.

A Polynesian sailor

The island groups of Melanesia, Micronesia, and Polynesia lie scattered across a vast area of the Pacific Ocean, to the east of Indonesia, New Guinea, Australia, and New Zealand. Around 3,500 years ago, the only islands in the region that were inhabited were those at its western edge, including what are today the Solomon and Admiralty islands. By A.D. 1000, however, almost every island had been reached and many had settled populations.

The people who achieved this remarkable feat sailed in dugout canoes made from large logs and driven by sails made of woven palm leaves. They traveled across hundreds — and sometimes thousands — of miles of open ocean, using the positions of the sun and stars to guide them. They also made navigation charts out of thin strips of wood and cowrie shells; the wooden strips showed ocean currents and winds, while the shells marked the positions of islands.

While at sea, the voyagers ate food they had taken with them. This included fruits, breadfruit, taro (a root vegetable grown in Southeast Asia), poultry, and dried shellfish. Fresh fish were caught on the journey, and drinking water was collected when it rained.

The Polynesians' canoes

The first Polynesian canoe consisted of a hollowed-out tree trunk attached to an outrigger — a small, boat-shaped float fixed by ropes and poles to one side of the canoe. This gave the canoe extra stability. Some canoes were built with two outriggers, one on each side of the hull. The sides of the canoe were raised to help protect passengers from the wind and waves. When storms threatened, a woven cover could be pulled over the hull.

Some of the later voyages, which carried settlers to the islands of eastern Polynesia, were probably made in double canoes, rather than canoes with outriggers. These were constructed from two large dugouts joined together by a number of curved wooden supports. A raised platform, large enough to carry up to thirty passengers and their belongings, was fixed to the top of the supports. The largest of these double canoes were 60-80 ft long.

Polynesian colonists sailed their canoes across thousands of miles of open ocean and spread their culture throughout the islands of the South Pacific Ocean.

The settlers who spread throughout the islands of the southern Pacific were descendants of the Lapita peoples of Indonesia, New Guinea, and western Melanesia. When they began to travel beyond these regions, they took with them all the things they would need to begin a new life in an uninhabited land. They loaded their canoes with tools made from stone, shell, and obsidian (volcanic glass). Livestock traveled with them too, including pigs, dogs, and poultry. Seed plants were also taken, to enable the settlers to grow coconuts, breadfruit, bananas, and root vegetables, such as yams and taro. Fish was an important part of their diet, and so the settlers carried a supply of fishhooks made from shells. Ornaments of shell and intricately carved red pottery were also stowed on board.

When they were out of sight of land, the sailors navigated by the stars in the night sky. They also watched ocean currents, winds, and the types of fish, which told them when they might be close to land. The flight course of land-living birds, the clouds that often form over islands in the ocean, and even the smell of land enabled them to pinpoint a likely destination.

When they reached a new island, the families of settlers would unload their possessions and set about building low thatched houses for shelter. Then they began their new life farming, fishing, and tending their animals, just as they had done previously but now in a new setting. This pattern of settlement was repeated time and again as more and more islands were occupied. Sometimes the settlers were forced to adapt their way of life to cope with different climates and soils.

The first islands to be reached and settled in this

A Polynesian fishhook carved out of shell. Colonists used hooks like this to catch fish while on their voyages.

Easter Island: a Polynesian mystery

After A.D. 400, when the first Polynesian settlers arrived, the population of Easter Island increased gradually to around 7,000. In about A.D. 1000, the islanders began to quarry and carve huge stone statues, which they erected on stone platforms in various parts of the island. Polynesian settlers on some other islands constructed paved terraces and platforms for religious purposes, but the statues of Easter Island are unique.

From 1600, the population declined because the island could not produce enough food and timber. However, the end of the island's civilization seems to have been sudden and catastrophic, as many statues were left unfinished and partly buried. No one knows why the inhabitants of Easter Island carved their statues, nor what brought about the collapse of their culture.

Some of the statues carved by the inhabitants of Easter Island.

way, from about 1500 B.C., were those of southern and eastern Melanesia. Within 400 years almost all of them had been visited and were occupied by settlers. The islands of Tonga and Samoa, near the edge of Melanesia, were reached in about 1100 B.C. The settlers and their descendants remained there for almost 1,000 years, isolated from the rest of the world.

Still further to the east lay the triangle of Polynesia, with its hundreds of unpopulated islands. Around 200 B.C., some settlers ventured into this huge area for the first time. From Samoa they sailed almost due east to the Marquesas Islands. These became the center from which the rest of Polynesia was colonized during the 1,200 years that followed. The Hawaiian Islands, 2,200 mi to the northwest, were reached in about A.D. 400. In about A.D. 1000 people began to colonize New Zealand.

Below A Polynesian navigation chart made from thin wooden strips and cowrie shells. It is a map of part of the Pacific Ocean showing sea currents and the position of islands to help the sailors find their way.

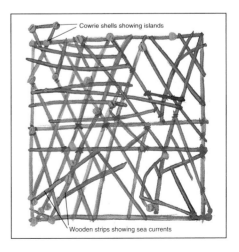

Cowrie shells showing islands

Wooden strips showing sea currents

A Roman sailor

Roman warships were powered by both a sail and oars. Most had three banks of oars, arranged one above another, and each oar was rowed by one or two men. The Greeks and Phoenicians – who were major powers in the Mediterranean before the Romans – had often used slaves as rowers. Roman

This mosaic shows a Roman warship. The eye on the bow was intended to frighten enemies.

oarsmen, however, were usually full-time members of the navy who had signed up to serve for 26 years or longer.

Warships were practical and there were no luxuries on board. There were no toilets and no kitchen; food had to be cooked on the shore when a ship stopped during its journey. The ships were also crowded, carrying up to 300 oarsmen, 120 soldiers, 2 steersmen, several other

sailors and the captain.

Before a ship went into battle, its mast and sail would be taken down. The oarsmen could achieve much greater speed and maneuver the ship better than by wind power. Sometimes the decks above the oarsmen were open to the air, and before going into battle a canvas cover was pulled across to protect the rowers from missiles fired or thrown from enemy ships.

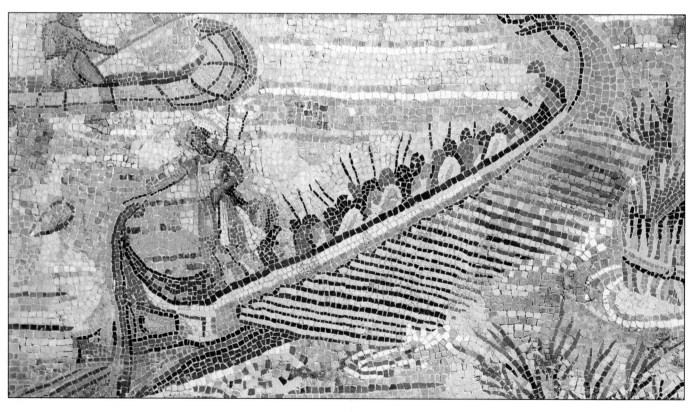

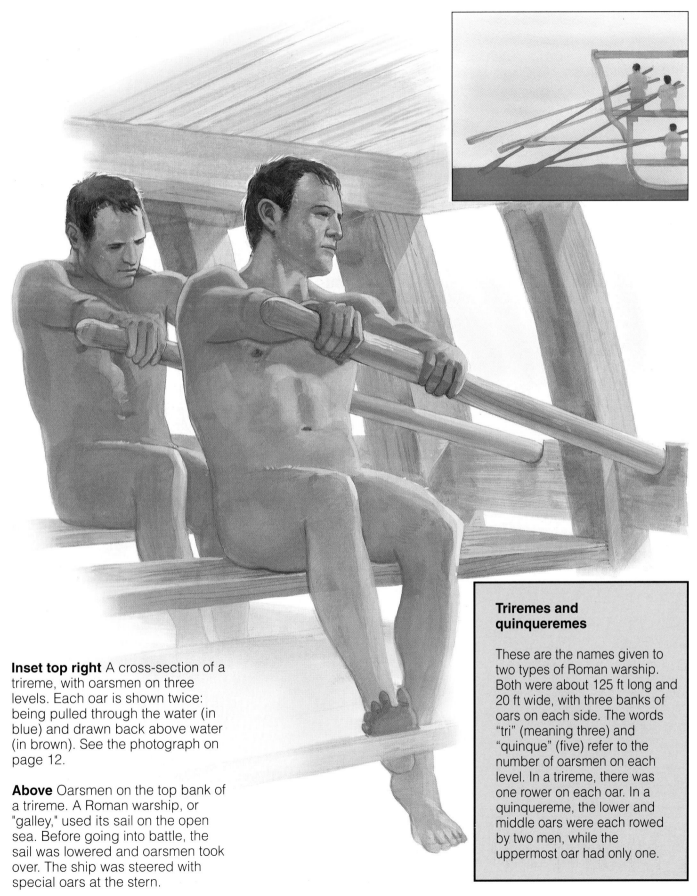

Inset top right A cross-section of a trireme, with oarsmen on three levels. Each oar is shown twice: being pulled through the water (in blue) and drawn back above water (in brown). See the photograph on page 12.

Above Oarsmen on the top bank of a trireme. A Roman warship, or "galley," used its sail on the open sea. Before going into battle, the sail was lowered and oarsmen took over. The ship was steered with special oars at the stern.

Triremes and quinqueremes

These are the names given to two types of Roman warship. Both were about 125 ft long and 20 ft wide, with three banks of oars on each side. The words "tri" (meaning three) and "quinque" (five) refer to the number of oarsmen on each level. In a trireme, there was one rower on each oar. In a quinquereme, the lower and middle oars were each rowed by two men, while the uppermost oar had only one.

It appears that the Romans did not have a fleet of warships until the First Punic War against the Carthaginians, which began in 264 B.C. Up to that time, all of Rome's wars had been fought on land. When they did begin to build ships, the Romans based their designs on those of the Phoenicians and Greeks. When a Carthaginian ship ran aground and fell into Roman hands, it too was used as a model for new warships.

Although they were latecomers to naval warfare, the Romans were very successful. Not only did they win a number of major sea battles, they also managed to rid the Mediterranean Sea of pirate ships by about 60 B.C., leaving the waters safe for their trading ships to sail.

In addition to triremes and quinqueremes, the Romans tried other warship designs. Some had only two banks of oars instead of three, and either one or two rowers to each oar. Others had three banks with two rowers on each oar; these "sixes," however, were normally used only as

A full-size replica of a Greek trireme at sea.

Battle tactics

The purpose of a Roman warship was to sink or overpower enemy ships. At the front of the ship, just below the waterline, was a sharp ram, tipped with metal. The oarsmen would attempt to sink another ship by rowing towards it at top speed and piercing it with the ram. If this failed, the soldiers on board would try to jump across to the enemy ship and defeat the crew in battle.

When a ship was holed by another's ram, it was often difficult for the crew to escape before the ship sank. Many oarsmen must have drowned in this way.

flagships in Roman fleets, not as fighting vessels. All of these ships needed highly skilled sailors. The 180 oarsmen on a trireme had to work in such a way that their oars all struck the water at the same time. If an oarsman made a mistake, his oar would interfere with others and this could cause chaos all along the ship. Oarsmen also had to be strong, as the oars were about 30 ft long and very heavy. Rowing at top speed must have been extremely hard work.

The Greeks had built ships even larger than "sixes." There are records of "twelves" with four rowers to each oar, and even a massive "forty" with gangs of thirteen or fourteen men pulling each oar. These larger ships had mostly disappeared by Roman times, although some "tens" were still in existence. In 31 B.C. the naval battle of Actium took place between two opposing fleets led by Mark Antony and Octavian, who were fighting for control of Rome. Mark Antony's fleet included some "tens," while Octavian's ships were probably lighter and faster quinqueremes. Octavian triumphed and made himself the first

Trading ships

Roman trading vessels were very different from warships. They were often larger — over 160 ft in length — and were powered only by sails. Some of the biggest had four separate holds in which cargoes could be stowed.

Among the goods shipped

A Roman trading ship unloading at Ostia.

around the Roman Empire were grain, gold, copper, silk, wine, spices, building stone, glass, and timber. Cargoes bound for Rome itself were unloaded at the seaport of Ostia and then sent by barge up the River Tiber to the city.

After Actium, Octavian became emperor of Rome.

emperor of Rome (known as Augustus). No ships larger than "sixes" were ever built again.

After Actium, Augustus strengthened his navy to protect trading ships carrying goods to and from Rome and between other parts of the Empire. Rome was by far the largest city and its population needed vast amounts of food, clothes, household items, and luxury goods. Some of these came from around the city, but most had to be imported. Although the Romans had a huge network of roads, these were used mainly by the army. It was far easier to transport cargoes by sea.

A Viking sailor

The Vikings lived in Scandinavia, in the countries we now call Denmark, Norway, and Sweden. They were at their most powerful from about A.D. 780 to 1070, when they sailed from their own lands and attacked many of the countries of western Europe.

Viking ships are known as longships because of their long, narrow shape. They were powered by oars and a sail. Each crewman had a sea chest in which he locked his possessions. The chest was also used as a seat when the man was rowing.

All the men were both sailors and soldiers; they sailed the ship and, when they reached their destination, they went into battle. They were not strangers to fighting. All Vikings were trained to use swords, shields, axes, spears, and bows and arrows from an early age.

When they went to sea, Vikings wore clothes that would keep them warm — linen undertrousers and

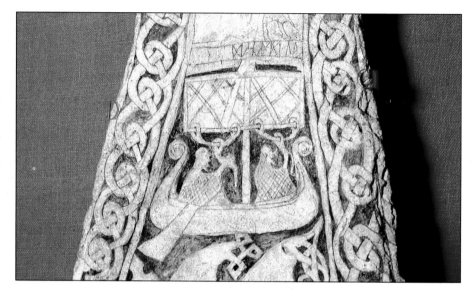

This Viking gravestone shows a longship and its warriors.

shirt, leather or woolen trousers, and a leather jerkin or fur-lined coat. Over these were waterproof garments made from oiled animal skins.

They also wore gloves, a woolen cap, and fur-lined leather boots. Battle helmets were made of leather, sometimes covered in iron. The sailors slept in leather sleeping bags, either on board the ship or on a beach.

Viking ships

The ships built by the Vikings were the most advanced of their time. The longships designed for raiding were fast, shallow craft, about 70 ft long and 17 ft wide, with about sixteen oars along each side. A fearsome dragon was often carved on the bow. Trading ships were built wider to carry plenty of cargo and had oars only at the bow and stern.

On the open sea in favorable winds, a longship was powered by a single square sail woven from coarse wool and dyed in bright colors. The mast was made from a sturdy pine tree trunk. Close to the shore, on rivers, or when the wind was unsuitable, the Vikings used oars. The ship was steered with a broad oar, attached near the stern on the right-hand side. This side became known as the steerboard, or starboard, side.

GREENLAND   ICELAND

IRELAND   RUSSIA

VINLAND

FRANCE

ITALY

Viking Routes

A Viking warrior wades ashore armed with an iron sword and wearing an iron helmet with gold decoration.

Vikings were feared by people living in coastal communities throughout Western Europe. They attacked swiftly, stole horses and food, took prisoners for slaves, and looted gold and silver from churches. The map shows the voyages made by Viking sailors.

Gold ornaments and jewelry made by Viking craftsmen.

Most Viking families lived by farming. They grew crops of rye, oats, wheat, barley, and vegetables, and kept cattle, sheep, pigs, and poultry to provide food, wool, skins, and feathers. They hunted wild animals, including boar, deer, bears, and rabbits, for their meat and skins.

When a farmer died, his land was inherited by his eldest son. Younger sons sometimes became craftsmen or traders in order to earn a living. The Vikings were excellent metal craftsmen and made beautiful jewelry and weapons from gold and silver. They were also expert wood carvers, and made many household objects from this abundant material. Most furniture was carved with intricate designs, and so were the Vikings' ships. In fact, their ships are some of the best examples of Viking craftsmanship.

Viking merchants sailed to Italy, Spain, France, Germany, Russia, and Iran, even traveling down the River Volga and crossing the Caspian Sea. They set out with cargoes of furs, walrus ivory, reindeer antlers and hides, amber, and slaves. They brought home gold, silver, jewels, wine, and textiles. Food, farm animals, and weapons were also traded. The Vikings seem to have traded quite peacefully but, as we know, they were not always peace-loving.

The name "Viking" comes from the old Norse language of Scandinavia, and it meant someone who came from a creek or sea inlet. To go "i viking" was to leave an inlet and go raiding. The Vikings did not set out on their raiding voyages because they were especially bloodthirsty — they went in search of new land and goods that they could not get by trading.

The prow of a Viking longship.

Most of Scandinavia is mountainous and the Vikings found that good farm land was in short supply. At first, farmers set out on raids to gain money to help support their families. They planted crops before they left and harvested them on their return; their families ran the farms while they were away. The first Viking raids were along the northeast and southwest coasts of England between A.D. 793 and 795. The raiders' main tactic was surprise. They went ashore and swiftly attacked towns, villages, and monasteries, killing the inhabitants and seizing their goods. Food, weapons, gold, silver, and other valuables were carried back to the longship and divided among the men.

Later, the problem of land shortage was made worse by long-running power struggles in which families often stole their neighbors' land. Eventually there was simply too little land to go around, and thousands of Viking families were forced to look for new places to live. They loaded their belongings, including animals, into boats and set off in search of a

Using only basic instruments, the Vikings were able to navigate in the open sea.

new home. From around 860, many Viking settlements sprang up in England, Scotland, Ireland, northern France, Finland, Iceland, and Greenland. One colony was even established in Newfoundland, off the coast of Canada. Most of these new territories were taken by conquest, but some were bought from the original occupants. The settlements founded by the Vikings were farming and trading communities, similar to those in their homeland.

Navigation

As well as being highly skilled shipbuilders, the Vikings were also expert navigators. They learned how to forecast the weather by looking at clouds. They studied the creatures and seaweed they saw, to tell whether they were close to land. They could also interpret differently colored areas of sea that might mean shallow water or rivers flowing into the sea.

Viking sailors did not have any maps or compasses. They navigated by the North Star at night. To help them stay on course during the daytime, they invented simple instruments that enabled them to calculate their course using the sun. The sun board had a dial marked with the compass points and was used to take a bearing from the rising or setting sun. A sun stone was a crystal that changed color when held at right angles to the sunlight, even when the sun was obscured by clouds. The shadow board was similar to a sundial but it was used to check the ship's course instead of the time.

A Portuguese sailor

During the fifteenth and early sixteenth centuries, European sailors crossed seas that were new to them and visited lands previously unknown to them. The mariners who began this age of exploration came from Portugal.

Starting in 1420 a Portuguese prince, known as Henry the Navigator, sent ships to explore the west coast of Africa. Henry made sure that his sailors were equipped with the best ships, instruments, and charts available.

The men themselves were often very experienced seafarers, although their knowledge was limited to the waters of the Mediterranean and the eastern Atlantic. After a brief period of training at Henry's school of navigation in Sagres, they were sent out into the unknown. To many this was a frightening idea. Some sailors believed that the seas off the African coast boiled and steamed; others said that the tides were so strong that no ship could ever return. They went, nonetheless, and they returned to Portugal with information about the lands they had visited. By the time Henry died

The city of Lisbon, from where many Portuguese expeditions set out to find new lands in the fifteenth and sixteenth centuries.

in 1460, his mariners had sailed as far south as Sierra Leone.

Christians and trade

There were two main reasons why Portuguese and Spanish rulers were so keen for their sailors to reach new lands. The first was trade. Although spices, silk, gold, and other goods from the East were sent overland to Europe, they passed through the hands of many Arab merchants on the way. At each stage the goods became more expensive. If Europeans could send ships to the lands where the goods were found, they would make enormous profits and cut the Arabs out of the trade.

The second reason was religion. Spanish and Portuguese monarchs were devoutly Christian, and they believed it was their duty to convert all "heathens" to Christianity.

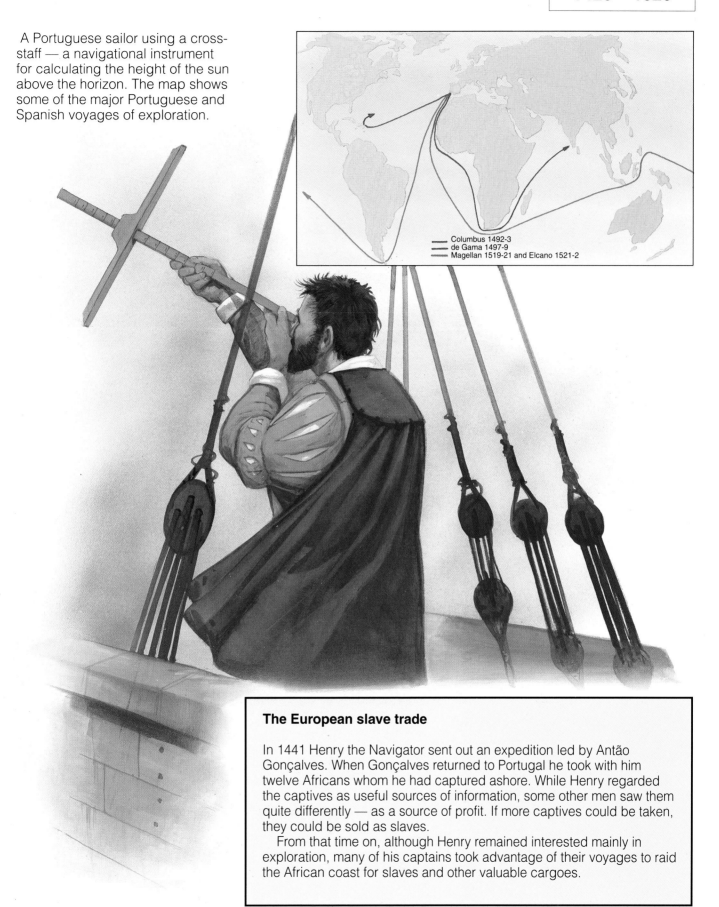

A Portuguese sailor using a cross-staff — a navigational instrument for calculating the height of the sun above the horizon. The map shows some of the major Portuguese and Spanish voyages of exploration.

Columbus 1492-3
de Gama 1497-9
Magellan 1519-21 and Elcano 1521-2

The European slave trade

In 1441 Henry the Navigator sent out an expedition led by Antão Gonçalves. When Gonçalves returned to Portugal he took with him twelve Africans whom he had captured ashore. While Henry regarded the captives as useful sources of information, some other men saw them quite differently — as a source of profit. If more captives could be taken, they could be sold as slaves.

From that time on, although Henry remained interested mainly in exploration, many of his captains took advantage of their voyages to raid the African coast for slaves and other valuable cargoes.

Portuguese exploration of the African coast dwindled after Henry the Navigator's death in 1460. In 1481, John II came to the throne and encouraged mariners to search farther south. His hope was that ships would be able to reach India, China, and the so-called Spice Islands, or Moluccas. The climax of John's reign came in 1487, when an expedition led by Bartholomew Diaz reached the southern tip of Africa. At that point, however, Diaz's crew mutinied and forced him to turn back.

Little progress was made in the years that followed. Then, in 1492, the Portuguese received a severe shock. Christopher Columbus, who was supported by Portugal's rival, Spain, claimed to have reached China by sailing westward across the Atlantic. Actually, he had landed on several islands in the Caribbean, but he and everyone else believed he had found a westward route to China. The Portuguese were outraged; they felt that exploration and the profitable trade that resulted from it were theirs by right.

Spain and Portugal were bitter rivals, but eventually they agreed on a compromise. In 1494 the Treaty of Tordesillas was signed. Under its terms, an imaginary north-south line was drawn through the Atlantic. All newly discovered lands to the west of the line were to belong to Spain, and Portugal would have those to the east.

By the time King Manuel I came to the Portuguese throne a year later, it was clear that Columbus had not reached China. The Portuguese decided to continue their search for an eastern route. In 1497 Vasco da Gama set sail from Lisbon; ten months later he anchored off the Indian port of Calicut. In the twenty years that followed, Portuguese expeditions visited many other territories which, according to the Treaty of Tordesillas, lay in their half of the world, including Brazil, the Philippines, Indonesia, and the Spice Islands. The Portuguese built up a very profitable trade with these countries and, as a result, became the wealthiest nation on earth.

Without doubt, the Portuguese mariners who sailed to these "new" lands were both skillful and daring. However, the credit for the greatest feat of seamanship must go to another Portuguese, sailing under the flag of Spain. In 1519 Ferdinand Magellan began an expedition that was to become the first voyage around the world.

Christopher Columbus on the first island he encountered in 1492.

He discovered a route from the Atlantic into the Pacific, around the southern tip of South America, thus succeeding where Columbus had failed. Magellan himself was killed during the voyage, and only one ship and eighteen men returned out of the five vessels and 287 sailors that had set out. Even so, the voyage was a remarkable achievement.

Magellan finds the route from the Atlantic Ocean into the Pacific.

Portuguese caravels

The ships with which Henry provided his sailors were the best vessels of the time, and were known as caravels. They were quite small — between 80 and 100 tons in weight and about 75 - 100 ft long. Most had two or three masts rigged with triangular sails. Caravels were not heavily armed, carrying only a few small guns and cannon for defense.

21

An Armada crewman

In the sixteenth century, life at sea was still harsh and dangerous. Worse still, this was a period of conflict. Naval battles could be extremely bloody: many sailors were killed or badly injured by cannon fire and flying shrapnel. Others fell overboard and were drowned, or were killed by enemy sailors who boarded their ship.

About half of the ship's crew often died during any long sea voyage — but not from gunshot wounds. Most were killed by diseases, especially scurvy, food poisoning, dysentery, and typhus. The main culprit was the food. The hold in which it was stored was deep in the ship, and was often infested with rats and mice. The meat was generally rotten, the ship's biscuit riddled with worms, and the drinking water green and evil-smelling. It is no surprise that very few men wanted to enlist in the navy for a long voyage. To make up the numbers needed on a ship, men were kidnapped by press gangs or threatened with imprisonment unless they went to sea.

This painting depicts the defeat of the Spanish Armada in 1588. In fact, severe storms did more damage than the English ships to the Spanish fleet.

Firing a cannon

First of all, the gun barrel had to be cleaned before the crew could pour in gunpowder and load the shot. Wadding was rammed into the barrel to hold everything in place. The master gunner then aimed the gun and one of the crew held a lighted taper to the touch hole at the rear of the barrel. The taper lit the gunpowder, which exploded and blew the shot out of the mouth of the gun.

The English could fire their guns three times as fast as the Spaniards. This was because English cannons were mounted on carriages with four wheels, making them quick and easy to move, load, and aim. The two-wheeled Spanish gun carriages were harder to maneuver.

An English gun crew firing their cannon during the battle of the Spanish Armada. Inset is a map showing the route taken by the Spanish fleet.

SCOTLAND

IRELAND

WALES

ENGLAND

Atlantic Ocean

SPANISH NETHERLANDS

FRANCE

Santander

PORTUGAL

SPAIN

Lisbon

A healthy diet?

The Spanish author of a humorous sixteenth-century book, *The Art of Sailing*, described the meat served on board ships of the time as follows: *"dried goat meat, quarters of sheep, salt beef and rusty bacon. This must be parboiled and not boiled, lightly burnt and not roasted, in such a way that, set on the table, it is loathsome to look at, hard as the devil to gnaw on, salty as hell to eat, indigestible as stones, and as harmful as rat poison if you eat your fill."*

The launching of the Spanish fleet, known as the Armada, in 1588 is the most famous naval event of the sixteenth-century. Relations between Spain and England had been getting worse for some years. Outright war was declared in 1585, when English troops were sent to help rebels in the Netherlands, which was a part of the Spanish empire.

On July 21, 1588, after two years of preparation, the Armada sailed from Spain. It was to link up with a strong army on the Dutch coast and escort the troops across the English Channel to invade England. The fleet was made up of 130 ships carrying 29,000 men. Having far fewer ships, the English dared not risk a direct attack, so they followed the Armada.

On August 6, the Spaniards anchored off the French port of Calais. The next night, the English attacked with fireships. These ships were filled with anything that would burn, then were set on fire and sent into the Spanish fleet, so that their flames would spread to the enemy's ships. Panicked, the Spanish captains ordered their men to cut

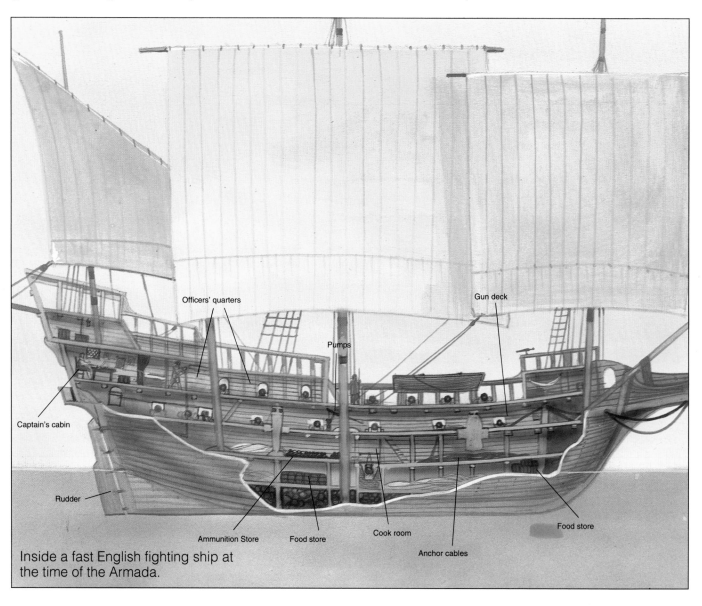

Officers' quarters

Gun deck

Pumps

Captain's cabin

Rudder

Ammunition Store

Food store

Cook room

Anchor cables

Food store

Inside a fast English fighting ship at the time of the Armada.

the anchor cables, so their ships would scatter with the wind. The following morning, the two fleets fought the Battle of Gravelines. For the first time, opposing ships came close enough for men to fire muskets at each other and to inflict serious damage with their heavy cannon.

After many hours of fighting, the fleets were separated by a sudden storm. The Spanish suffered very heavy losses. Nearly all of their large fighting ships were damaged and leaking, and hundreds of their men had been killed. Their ordeal was not yet over, however. Strong winds blew their remaining ships northward through the North Sea. The English gave chase at first, but then turned back.

The Spanish commanders decided to return to Spain by sailing around the coast of Scotland and southward to the west of Ireland. It was a nightmare journey. Food was short and what little there was had gone rotten; records of the voyage show that by August 21, 3,000 men were ill. The Spanish sailors had little knowledge of the treacherous waters around the rocky Irish coast, or the savage autumn

Francis Drake

In the years leading up to the Armada, one of the factors that worsened relations between Spain and England was the plundering of Spanish ships by English privateers. These sailors made a handsome living by attacking and robbing treasure ships returning to Spain from Spanish colonies in Central and South America. The most feared privateer was Francis Drake, a man with a burning hatred of Spaniards. Between 1572 and 1585, he stole millions of dollars worth of gold and silver from Spanish ships and colonies. He seemed to have a sixth sense that helped him locate treasure. The Spaniards believed he had a magic mirror in which he could see all of the world's oceans and the ships sailing on them.

storms that raged there. About twenty-five ships were wrecked and thousands of men drowned. Along a 10-mi stretch of the Irish coast, one English official counted "1,110 dead corpses of men which the sea had driven upon the shore." Most of the Spaniards who struggled on to dry land were killed by English soldiers stationed in Ireland.

About ninety Armada ships eventually made it back to Spain. But men on both sides continued to suffer, and many soon died of diseases they had caught during the campaign. In the end, around half of the men in the English fleet and two-thirds of those in the Armada had died.

The voyage of the *Mayflower*

On September 16, 1620, a small ship, the *Mayflower*, set sail from Plymouth, England, bound for America. There were 149 people on board — forty-seven officers and crew and 102 passengers, who planned to settle in the colony of Virginia, which had been founded thirteen years before.

The ship was loaded with furniture, household utensils, goats, and chickens — all necessary for starting life in a new country. There was also a plentiful supply of food, including salted beef, vegetables, bread, and beer.

Because of bad weather and a rather incompetent navigator, the *Mayflower* did not arrive in Virginia. On Christmas Day 1620, the settlers landed instead to the north, in Cape Cod Bay. There was almost no food to eat. To make matters worse, they arrived in the frozen depths of winter.

They built log huts and a small wooden fort for protection, and named their settlement Plymouth. They could find little to eat other than oysters and clams from the sea. Already weakened after their voyage, the settlers suffered terribly from the cold, starvation, and scurvy. Within a few months almost half of them had died.

The *Mayflower* leaves Plymouth.

The conditions in which the colonists lived aboard the *Mayflower* were very cramped. Their journey was made even more uncomfortable by frequent storms. The settlers finally came ashore in Cape Cod Bay, far north of their intended destination .

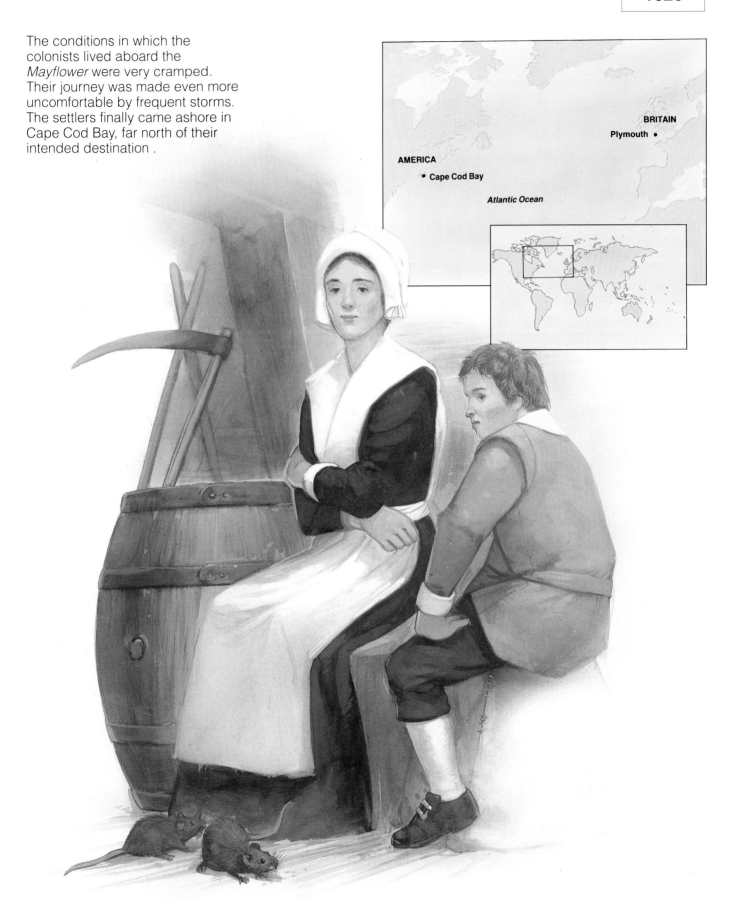

BRITAIN

Plymouth •

AMERICA

• Cape Cod Bay

Atlantic Ocean

The Pilgrims landed in Cape Cod Bay, Massachusetts, on Christmas Day in 1620.

The settlers who arrived in America aboard the *Mayflower* have come to be known as the Pilgrims. These men, women, and children were Puritans who believed that the Church of England had corrupted the Christian faith, and they wanted to worship God in their own way. Their ideas were opposed by the Church of England and the King: King James I had threatened religious dissenters that he would "make them conform or … harry them out of the land."

Some Puritans had indeed been harried out of England in 1608, and had gone to Leyden in the Netherlands, where their faith was tolerated. About thirty-five of these so-called Separatists left Leyden to join the *Mayflower* in 1620. The rest of the passengers were members of other dissenting religious sects from London and Southampton.

In an attempt to ensure that peace and order were maintained among the various groups, a document called the *Mayflower* Compact was drawn up and signed by all the men of the new community. They agreed to "covenant and combine" themselves into a "civil Body Politick" in order to make "just and equal Laws." In doing so they were proclaiming their right to govern themselves.

The Pilgrims found that the Wampanoag people were living near the area they had decided to settle. The Wampanoag people helped the settlers by showing them how to grow corn in the poor soil of the region, and the

This painting shows Puritans leaving Delft in the Netherlands to join the *Mayflower*.

The Wampanoag people showed the European settlers how to cultivate corn for food.

Wampanoag leader, Massasoit, made a peace treaty with the settlers. Even so, life was far from easy. Yet not one of the survivors went with the *Mayflower* when it returned to England the following summer. Instead they sent a letter urging others to join them: "The country wanteth only industrious men to employ. For it would grieve your hearts if you had seen so many miles, by good rivers, uninhabited."

This call was answered and more settlers did arrive. Many of them were Puritans, though few were as strongly opposed to the Church of England as the Pilgrims were. In 1630, 500 men, women, and children arrived and founded a settlement at Massachusetts Bay. They attracted many more immigrants and, within ten years, their community grew to between 15,000 and 20,000. They were more successful than the earlier settlers. As well as raising cattle, corn, and vegetables to feed themselves, they soon became involved in selling fish and furs to merchants in England and other parts of Europe. However, as the settlement grew larger the people already living in the area — the Wampanoag and the Narraganset — fought to keep their lands. They were defeated by the settlers, and many died from the European diseases they brought with them (like measles and smallpox).

The townships around

Shortly after the *Mayflower* arrived in America, one of the settlers wrote: *"Being thus passed the vast ocean... they had now no friends to welcome them, nor inn to entertaine or refresh their weatherbeaten bodys, no houses and much less townes to repaire too... [and] it was muttered by some that if they got not a place in time they would turn... their goods ashore [and return]."* (Quoted by Alistair Cooke, *America*, 1973, p. 78.)

Massachusetts Bay united to become Massachusetts. Other colonies — Rhode Island, Connecticut, Maine, New Hampshire, and Vermont — grew up to the north and south. Although the climate was more extreme and the land more forested than in England, the colonies had so much in common with the "mother country" that together they became known as New England.

From sail to steam

From the earliest times boats have been propelled through the water by paddles, oars, and sails. At the start of the nineteenth century, however, a new type of power was tried — steam.

At first, most people regarded steam-powered ships as a passing fancy. Even the men who designed them seemed unsure: many early vessels had masts and sails, as well as steam boilers and paddle wheels. Gradually, though, as faster ships and more efficient engines were developed, steamships challenged and then replaced sailing ships on most sea routes.

As a result, the lives of many sailors were changed. In the days of sail, sailors spent a great deal of time on deck, setting the sails to catch as much of the wind's energy as possible. The age of steam shifted the focus of activity below deck, to the engine room. Now seamen had to ensure that the furnaces were fed with enough coal and that the

The first successful steam-powered ship, *Charlotte Dundas.*

engines kept working. A new hazard was added to those already faced by sailors. In the early days of steam, it was not uncommon for boilers to explode and many men were killed by such accidents.

Paddle wheels and propellers

Steamships built during the first forty years of the nineteenth century were moved through the water by large paddle wheels, fitted one on each side of the ship. As the wheels turned, they pushed against the water, forcing the ship forward. In 1836, the first successful propeller-driven steamship was built. Propellers were more efficient than paddle wheels — they needed less power from the engines to move a ship at the same speed.

By 1845 the propeller was widely accepted. Paddle wheels were still used, however. When Isambard Kingdom Brunel built the *Great Eastern* in 1858, he equipped it with two 56-ft paddle wheels, a 24-ft propeller, and six masts with over 6,400 square yards of sail.

Steamships needed coal to fuel their engines. On large ships, an army of stokers was employed to shovel coal into the furnaces that heated the steam boilers.

The main drawback of wind power and sails is that the wind itself is unreliable. Frequently it blows too strongly from the wrong direction, taking ships way off course, or not at all, leaving them becalmed, sometimes for days. Steamships promised to put an end to these problems. The first successful steam-powered ship was the *Charlotte Dundas*, built in 1803 to operate on the Forth and Clyde Canal in Scotland. Thirteen years later, the first passenger steamship service began, between the British resort, Brighton, and Le Havre, on the northern coast of France.

Most people, however, regarded steamships as little more than an interesting novelty. On long trade routes, such as across the Atlantic or from the United States to the Far East, merchants continued to use sailing ships. They knew they could rely on regular sailings and could usually predict, within a day or two, when the ships would arrive. Furthermore, on Far East trade routes there was a shortage of places where steamships could take on more coal. Also, early steam engines often broke down on long voyages.

Some builders of sailing ships recognized the threat posed by steam. They realized that in order to compete, they had to design faster sailing ships. In 1845 John Griffiths and Donald McKay launched the *Rainbow*. It had a long, sleek hull that brought jeers from more traditional shipbuilders, who were convinced that the vessel was too light and that its sharply pointed bow would dive beneath the waves. Their laughter died away when the *Rainbow* completed its first run from New York to Hong Kong in a record ninety-two days.

In the following year, Griffiths built the *Sea Witch*, the first of the so-called "clippers." These ships achieved high speeds because of their sleek design and

The clippers *Ariel* and *Taeping* racing to England with their cargoes of China tea in 1866.

their vast array of sails on tall masts – 32 sails was not uncommon. In 1849, *Sea Witch* sailed from Hong Kong to New York in seventy-four days, a record that has never been broken by a sailing ship.

Clippers required a special kind of seaman to sail them. In bad weather, when the order "Aloft and furl!" was shouted, some of the crew had to climb to the top of the masts to take in the sails. Then they had to ride aloft through the wind and rain until the storm died down.

Despite their speed and beauty, the clippers' days were numbered. Steamships became steadily faster, more efficient, and cheaper to operate. In 1865 the steamer *Ajax* sailed the 8,400 mi from Liverpool to Mauritius and back without refueling. Then, in 1869, the Suez Canal was opened. It cut out the long journey around the southern tip of Africa, reducing the sea route from Britain to India and the Far East by 3,400 mi. Within a few years the valuable cargoes that previously had been sent by clipper were being carried by steamships.

A poster advertising a clipper ship bound from New York to San Francisco in 1850.

Precious cargoes

Although they were very fast, clippers could not carry huge amounts of cargo. They were used to ship only very valuable goods. Tea from China and India was one such cargo, and each year there were races between clippers striving to bring the first of the new crop to Britain.

When gold was discovered in California in 1849, prospectors clamored to get aboard clippers sailing from the east coast. Although the ships had to sail around Cape Horn, they were still the quickest and safest means of getting to the other side of the continent. This sea route declined rapidly after 1869, when the first transcontinental railway was completed.

The discovery of gold in Australia in 1851 also attracted prospectors. Once again, clippers were the fastest way for people to travel there and return with their gold.

Ships passing through the newly opened Suez Canal.

A liner crewman

When the passenger liner *Mauretania* was launched in 1907, it was the largest ship afloat, measuring 790 ft long by 88 ft wide and weighing 36,400 tons. A total of 2,165 passengers (563 in first class, 464 in second, and 1,138 in third) could be carried across the Atlantic between Britain and the U. S.

The *Mauretania* was powered by four huge steam turbine engines. An army of stokers was needed to feed coal into the furnaces which turned water to steam in the ship's boilers. Besides the stokers and other seamen who actually sailed the ship, large numbers of crew were required to look after the passengers. There were cooks, stewards, cleaners, musicians, and many others. In all the crew totaled 812.

There was strong competition on the Atlantic route, and shipping companies tried hard to attract passengers away from rival ships. The *Mauretania* was designed to be the fastest ship on the route, and it soon lived up to expectations. On the return journey from New York to Liverpool, it broke the record, with a time of 4 days, 22 hours, and 29 minutes.

Luxury afloat

The *Mauretania* was luxurious as well as fast — especially for those passengers who could afford to travel first class. There were panels of polished mahogany, delicate carvings, a library modeled on the architectural style of eighteenth-century France, grand staircases, and elevators — the first on any British ship.

New ocean liners were always featured in the newspapers of the time, and journalists pronounced the *Mauretania* the most magnificent ship afloat. On its maiden voyage, however, it became clear that there was a price to pay for high speed — the *Mauretania* rattled loudly!

The *Mauretania,* one of the most famous Atlantic liners.

Liverpool
BRITAIN
Atlantic Ocean
USA
New York

Many of the crew aboard an ocean liner were employed to look after the passengers — cooking and serving food and drinks, providing entertainment, and cleaning the ship. The map shows one of the main liner routes across the Atlantic between Liverpool, England, and New York.

The age of the steam liner began in 1833, when the *Royal William* became the first ship to cross the Atlantic under steam power alone. The voyage from Picton, Nova Scotia, to the Isle of Wight took twenty-one days. Five years later the *Great Western*, built by the engineer Isambard Kingdom Brunel, cut the journey to fourteen days — eight less than the fastest sailing ship — and began a regular service. The fare of $50.00 for a cabin and food was felt to be very expensive, but there was no shortage of passengers willing to pay for a fast crossing.

These early steam liners were made of wood and driven by paddle wheels. In 1843 Brunel launched the *Great Britain* — the first large iron ship and the first ocean-going vessel to be powered by a propeller.

During the next few years, liners steadily grew larger. Then, in 1854, Brunel began building the *Great Eastern*, which he planned to be far bigger than any other ship. When launched, it weighed over 21,000 tons, compared to its nearest rival at just under 4,400 tons. The vessel cost an enormous amount of money to build and run, and could not attract enough customers to pay its way. On its maiden voyage there were 412 crew on board and just thirty-eight paying passengers.

The *Great Eastern* made its owners bankrupt and its many complications sent Brunel to an early grave. Later, however, it was put to good use laying the first telegraph cables across the

Isambard Kingdom Brunel's steamship the *Great Eastern*. It was powered by means of paddle wheels, a propeller, and sails.

Brunel, who built the *Great Western* and the *Great Eastern*.

Atlantic. Meanwhile, other shipping companies were establishing themselves and making money on the Atlantic passenger route. Among them was Cunard, owned by Samuel Cunard, a Canadian who had been one of the shareholders in the *Royal William*. The Cunard line grew, building ever-larger and faster

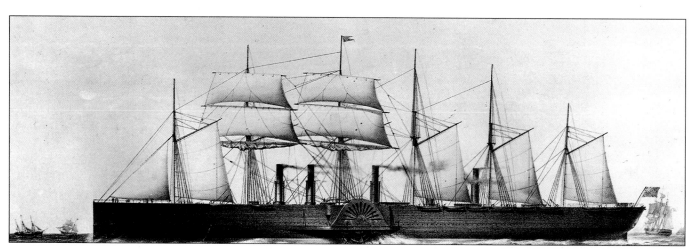

ships. By 1893 its ships *Campania* and *Lucania* had cut the crossing time to five and a half days.

In 1909 the *Mauretania* did the Liverpool to New York run in just 4 days,10 hours, and 51 minutes, a record that remained unbroken until 1929. The heyday of the great ocean liners came in the 1930s, with the launching of the *Queen Mary* in 1934 and *Queen Elizabeth* in 1938. In just 100 years, liners had grown from the 1,450 tons of the *Great Western* to the *Queen Elizabeth's* 92,900 tons. Both the

Above The *Queen Mary* enters New York on her maiden voyage in 1934.

Speed at any price?

On April 10, 1912, the steamship *Titanic* set out from Southampton bound for New York. The ship's owners wanted to capture the Blue Riband (an award for the fastest crossing of the Atlantic) from the *Mauretania*. The *Titanic* was larger and even more luxurious than its rival, and was believed to be unsinkable.

Four days into the journey, the captain was warned of the danger of icebergs. Fearlessly, he steamed on through thick fog. Just before midnight, a large iceberg was spotted in the *Titanic's* path. The ship could not stop in time and the iceberg ripped a hole in the prow.

When the time came to abandon the sinking ship, it was discovered that there were not enough lifeboats. The *Titanic* sank at 2:00 a.m.; 1,513 people drowned.

"Queens" were converted into troop carriers during the Second World War and became most attractive targets for enemy German U-boat (submarine) captains. However, their speed helped them to survive.

The end of the war in 1945 was also the beginning of the end for the great liners. Long-distance jet aircraft had arrived, and they soon began carrying passengers. By 1960 nearly 70 percent of people who crossed the Atlantic went by airplane.

A U-boat crewman

During the Second World War, which lasted from 1939 to 1945, German submarines, or U-boats, hunted British and American merchant ships in the Atlantic Ocean. Their aim was to sink as many as possible, in order to prevent much-needed supplies from reaching Britain.

U-boats were designed only for war, and the men who served on them lived in very uncomfortable conditions. The boats were cramped, with stores stacked in every available space. Clothing was kept wherever there was room, for example stuffed behind pipes. The stench of oil fuel and human bodies was overpowering; in bad weather, it was made worse by seasickness. Although the German navy gave its submariners the best food available, cooking was not possible when a submarine was underwater. Then the crew had to satisfy their hunger with spicy sausages, which were stored hanging from the ceiling.

Voyages often lasted several months, and boredom was a major problem. Nervousness replaced boredom when a U-boat sighted a target and went into attack. Early in the war U-boats could attack at will, but gradually

A submariner's-eye view of a ship torpedoed by a U-boat.

Allied ships devised ways of fighting back. A great many U-boats were sunk during the Second World War, and nearly 30,000 German submariners were killed.

Life below

"Life aboard is monotonous for long periods. For many long weeks one must be able to bear failures, and when depth charges are added, life becomes a war of nerves ... Life aboard a submarine is unnatural and unhealthy... there is no constant change between day and night for the lights have to burn all the time ... there is no regular time for sleeping since most of the fighting is done at night." (Wolfgang Lueth, a U-boat captain, talking to fellow naval officers in 1943. Quoted by Richard Compton-Hall, *The Underwater War, 1939-1945*, 1982, p. 30.)

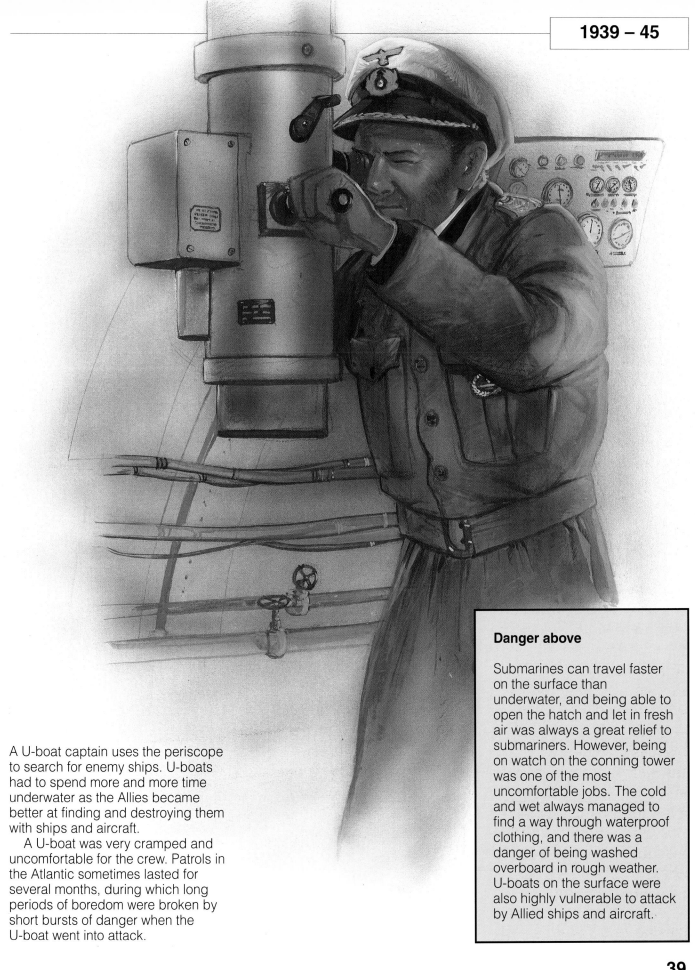

A U-boat captain uses the periscope to search for enemy ships. U-boats had to spend more and more time underwater as the Allies became better at finding and destroying them with ships and aircraft.

A U-boat was very cramped and uncomfortable for the crew. Patrols in the Atlantic sometimes lasted for several months, during which long periods of boredom were broken by short bursts of danger when the U-boat went into attack.

Danger above

Submarines can travel faster on the surface than underwater, and being able to open the hatch and let in fresh air was always a great relief to submariners. However, being on watch on the conning tower was one of the most uncomfortable jobs. The cold and wet always managed to find a way through waterproof clothing, and there was a danger of being washed overboard in rough weather. U-boats on the surface were also highly vulnerable to attack by Allied ships and aircraft.

The first submarine used in war was the *Turtle* in 1776, during the Revolutionary War.

Following Britain's declaration of war against Germany in September 1939, large numbers of merchant ships began sailing across the Atlantic from the U.S. to Britain. They carried essential supplies of weapons, oil, and food. The Germans thought that if they could sink enough of these ships, Britain would be forced to surrender.

The merchant ships often traveled in groups, or convoys, and were only lightly protected by warships, which could do little to fight off attacks. Once a convoy had been located by one or more U-boats, it was only a matter of time before German torpedoes struck.

Attacks were usually carried out at night in the hope of keeping the submarine out of sight for as long as possible. U-boats moved in, on the surface, to within a few hundred yards before firing their torpedoes. This was risky for the submarine itself, particularly if it was spotted early in the attack, but it made aiming the torpedoes easier.

A U-boat was armed with about twelve torpedoes, which were fired from tubes in the bow and stern. Each torpedo carried a warhead of between 600 and 800 pounds of high explosive that could sink a ship within a matter of seconds. Not all torpedoes worked properly, however. Some went off course or passed beneath their target; others hit but failed to explode. In addition to their torpedoes, submarines had one or two guns mounted on deck. They were used to "finish off" damaged ships, but only when there was little risk of the submarine itself being attacked.

At first the U-boats were very successful. During the first three years of the war, 3,862 Allied merchant ships were sunk for the

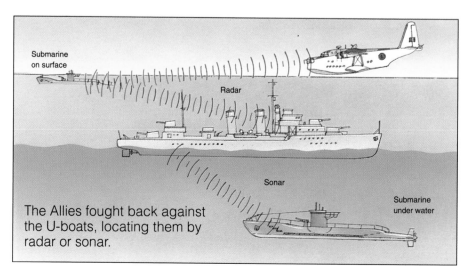

The Allies fought back against the U-boats, locating them by radar or sonar.

loss of just 152 U-boats. The following year the tide turned in the Allies' favor. Attack planes based on aircraft carriers, long-range patrol aircraft, well-equipped escort ships, and improved anti-submarine tactics took a heavy toll on the U-boats, forcing them to patrol and attack while submerged. This made the submarines far less effective. In 1943, 237 U-boats were destroyed while only 597 merchant ships were sunk.

The main weapons used against submarines were depth charges — large canisters of high explosive set to detonate at a certain depth in the water. A depth charge that detonated within about 30 ft of a submarine was usually lethal, but serious damage could be caused by explosions at greater range. When under attack, U-boats dived as deep as they could. Silence was then vital, as any sound might give away the submarine's position and make it easy for the enemy to score a direct hit. U-boats sometimes fired a mixture of oil and rubbish from their torpedo tubes to make it appear that they had been sunk, but this trick rarely worked.

In for the kill

U-boat captains were encouraged to take risks in order to increase their chances of sinking enemy ships. The Commanding Officers' Handbook instructed them to: *"dive only when an immediate hazardous fight is expected ... serious miscalculations may occur at night, therefore go in as close as possible ... keep your nerve and do not fire too soon ... distance is easily underestimated ... one is always farther away than one thinks, particularly at night. Stick it out and go nearer..."*

A lookout on the conning tower of a U-boat in 1942.

Attack from the air

U-boats on the surface were vulnerable to aircraft, which could arrive on the scene and attack far more quickly than ships. Submarine captains ordered their vessels to dive at the first sign of any aircraft, whether or not it presented a threat. As a result, perhaps the major effect of anti-submarine aircraft was that U-boat crews could never relax and they eventually became exhausted.

A supertanker crewman

Since the early 1960s ships have been powered by diesel. The largest merchant ships afloat today are huge supertankers known as ULCCs, or Ultra Large Crude Carriers. These vessels are used to carry crude oil from the areas in which it is found to the places where it is processed and used.

Despite its size, a ULCC does not have a very large crew. Many of its operations are controlled by computers; only about forty seamen are needed. They have to be extremely well-trained to sail such a large and complex vessel. Some crewmen spend much of their free time studying subjects related to their work, such as electronics, engineering, navigation, and automatic control systems.

The crew of a supertanker live in air-conditioned quarters and have good food to eat. To relax they can swim in the ship's pool, go to the library on board, watch film shows, or visit the games room. When crew members fall ill, they can usually be treated in the ship's own hospital. Because voyages can last many weeks, one of the worst problems faced by the crew is boredom.

Staying on course

When a supertanker is at sea, it is kept on course by an automatic pilot. Radio navigation equipment picks up signals from transmitters around the world and calculates the ship's exact position. Computers compare this information with the ship's planned course, and move the rudder if any correction is needed. In coastal waters or when approaching a port, the crew take manual control of the vessel.

Electronic instruments in the control room constantly check that the engines are working properly. Other devices measure the temperature throughout the ship, including the holds where the oil is stored, and warn if anything is wrong.

Some supertankers are so large that in calm weather the crew use bicycles to get from one end of the ship to the other. In rough seas, when waves break over the deck, crew members walk along a raised gangway.

A modern supertanker at sea.

The name Ultra Large Crude Carrier is used for a supertanker that can carry over 330,000 tons of crude oil. Because of their size, these ships can operate only on a few ocean routes — from the Arabian Gulf to North America, Europe, and the Far East. Even when empty, they are too big to pass through the Suez Canal. To reach Europe or North America, they have to sail around the southern tip of Africa.

Not many ports are large enough to accommodate a ULCC, so oil is often loaded at special terminals several miles offshore. It is pumped into a number of separate tanks in the ship. This prevents the cargo from slopping around in heavy seas, which might make the ship unstable. It also means that if the ship is damaged in an accident, only those tanks that have been pierced will leak, not the entire load of oil.

Crude oil burns fiercely when it is ignited, so the temperature of the cargo has to be monitored carefully. The main hazard is not the oil itself but the highly explosive fumes it gives off. A serious explosion could blow the ship apart, so a great deal of the complex electronic equipment on board is designed to make sure that this never happens.

Supertanker accidents do occur, however, and sometimes vast quantities of oil are spilled into the sea. Not all oil pollution is accidental, though. When a tanker has unloaded its oil, the tanks must be cleaned out before another load is

Oil disaster

The worst oil-tanker accident in recent years occurred in 1989, when the *Exxon Valdez* ran aground in Prince William Sound, on the coast of Alaska. More than 11 million gallons of crude oil spilled from its tanks, creating a slick covering about 100 sq mi. This much oil could not be contained quickly by booms, and when it washed ashore it covered over 1,200 mi of shoreline.

Although efforts were made to clean up the coast afterwards, these came too late to prevent widespread damage. Thousands of sea birds, whales, sea otters, salmon, herring, and shellfish died, and many fishing communities lost their livelihood.

The *Exxon Valdez* disaster.

taken on board. Powerful jets of water are sprayed into the tanks and the mixture of oil and water is then pumped into a "slop" tank to be emptied later. Sometimes tankers pump the oil and water straight into the sea, even though this is illegal.

Vital Statistics

The largest supertanker ever built is the *Seawise Giant*, constructed in Japan in 1979. It measures 1,500 ft from bow to stern and can carry 620,000 tons of crude oil.

Apart from supertankers, there are many different types of merchant ships at work today. Some tankers are specially built to carry gas — generally in liquefied form to take up less space. Bulk cargo carriers have large, box-shaped holds to take loose solid cargoes, such as cement, grain, coal, fertilizers, or iron ore.

Many solid cargoes are now shipped in containers. These are large metal boxes, made in a range of standard sizes, which can be loaded and unloaded much more quickly than

Containers are widely used because they can be transferred easily between trucks, docks, and ships.

loose cargoes. The use of containers, which began in the late 1950s, has changed the way in which many cargoes are handled at ports. Containers are loaded and unloaded by huge cranes, sorted, and then lifted on to trucks or freight cars to be transported elsewhere. Much of the process is controlled by computers, and very few people are needed.

45

Glossary

Allies The countries that fought against Germany, Italy, and Japan during the Second World War. The main Allied powers were Britain, the United States, and the Soviet Union.

Armada A fleet of armed ships.

Becalmed Unable to move because of lack of wind.

Boom A floating barrier.

Bow The front end of a ship.

Carthage An ancient city in North Africa on the Bay of Tunis. It was destroyed by the Romans in 146 B.C.

Colony A community formed by people in a country far away from their homeland. Colonists usually kept strong links with the country from which they came.

Conning tower The structure above the deck of a submarine, used as the bridge from which the vessel is piloted when it is on the surface.

Diesel A type of engine in which fuel is ignited at a constant pressure in a cylinder.

Dissenter A person who refuses to worship in the way laid down by an established church.

Dysentery A serious stomach infection, usually caught by taking in food and water contaminated with germs.

Harry To harrass or worry someone to force them to do what you want.

Hull The main body of a ship.

Mahogany A dark hardwood obtained from a tropical tree species.

Maneuver To move in a complicated way to confuse an enemy.

Musket An early type of handgun.

Mutinied Rebelled against the authority of the ship's captain.

Navigation The process of planning the route of a ship or aircraft and keeping it on course.

Phoenicians The people of a Middle Eastern civilization who inhabited the region of Syria around 1500 B.C.

Press gang A group of men who forced civilians to enlist in the navy or join a ship for a long voyage.

Privateer A crewman aboard a privately owned ship fighting on behalf of a government. Francis Drake, for example, attacked Spanish ships and ports on the authority of Queen Elizabeth I.

Prow Another name for the bow, or front, of a ship.

Scurvy A disease caused by lack of vitamin C. Before its cause was discovered, sailors on long voyages often caught scurvy because they did not eat enough fresh fruit and vegetables that contain vitamin C.

Ship's biscuit A hard biscuit eaten by sailors on long voyages to give them energy.

Spice Islands An old name for the Moluccas, a group of island in the Far East where valuable spices were grown.

Steam turbine A type of engine in which steam is generated in a boiler and is used to drive a turbine. The turbine has a rotor with blades, and when the steam hits the blades, it pushes against them, turning the rotor.

Stern The back end of a ship.

Steward A waiter on a ship or aircraft.

Stoker A person employed to shovel coal into a furnace.

Stores Cloting, food, and other supplies necessary to life at sea.

Suez Canal The canal linking the Mediterranean Sea with the Red Sea, opened in 1869.

Supertanker Any tanker that can carry more than 80,000 tons of cargo.

Torpedo A cylindrical weapon that can be launched from a submarine, ship, or aircraft. It has its own engine and contains a high explosive which detonates when the torpedo hits an enemy ship.

Typhus A highly infectious disease.

U-boat The short from of Unterseeboot, the German word for submarine (under-the-sea boat).

Further reading

Ballard, Robert D. *The Lost Wreck of the Isis: From Beneath the Sea—An Ancient Roman Ship.* New York: Scholastic, 1990.

Humble, Richard. *Ships: Sailors and the Sea.* New York: Franklin Watts, 1991.

———*U-Boat.* New York: Franklin Watts, 1990.

———*World War I Battleship.* New York: Franklin Watts, 1989.

———*World War II Aircraft Carrier.* New York: Franklin Watts, 1989.

Mulvihill, Margaret. *Viking Longboats.* New York: Gloucester Press, 1989.

The Visual Dictionary of Ships and Sailing. New York: Dorling Kindersley, 1991.